Welcome to the Pleasuredome . . .

THE Eighties marked a new, no-nonsense approach to government, the birth of the Yuppie, and the final collapse of Communism in Eastern Europe.

Technology and society were rapidly changing. We were told that 'greed is good' and were driven by the need to succeed, in a world where it seemed that the rich got richer and the poor got poorer.

It was a time of radical social change, of marvel and maelstrom, when we shared visions of revolution and nuclear paranoia in equal measure.

In the 1980s there was no more political city to grow up in than Liverpool. The people fought against unemployment, Degsy took control of the city's propaganda machine, and the Toxteth riots put Liverpool in headlines all over the world.

There was also regeneration of the city's landscape on a huge scale – the Albert Dock was reborn and the Cavern Quarter echoed to the swinging sound of success. Liverpool ruled the charts with a new wave of Mersey Beat musicians, and on stage and screen Alan Bleasdale and Willy Russell recast the city in a starring role.

It was a decade when football united us in tragedy. But we shared the joy when the greatest derby in the world came to Wembley. Proof, should it ever have been needed, that whatever divisions may exist in Liverpool, the proud people of a much-maligned city are united by their common love of sport.

Words: Vicky Andrews, Peter Grant

Photography: Liverpool Daily Post and Echo Archives

Picture Research: Colin Hunt, Brian Johnston, Leslie Rawlinson,

Design and Layout: Lee Ashun, Zoe Bevan, Adam Oldfield, Colin Sumpter

Published by: Trinity Mirror Merseyside, PO Box 48, Old Hall Street, Liverpool L69 3EB

Printed by: Pensord, Tram Road, Pontllanfraith, Blackwood NP12 2YA

ISBN: 978-1-906802-20-2

The music plays on –
the scene at the vigil
for John Lennon in
Liverpool

GRIEF FOR A WORKING CLASS HERO

THE world was stunned with grief when John Lennon was shot dead in New York on December 8, 1980.

Grief-stricken fans gathered in the cold of Mathew Street in Liverpool city centre when the news came through. The site of the Cavern became a shrine to his memory.

In New York, more than 5,000 people converged on the scene of Lennon's shooting, singing Beatles songs.

More than 25,000 people paid a final tribute in Liverpool to Lennon, the man of peace, on December 15. The biggest crowd of music lovers since the early days of Beatlemania gathered outside a windswept St George's Hall for a vigil.

At 7pm the tearful fans joined millions throughout the world in 10 minutes' silent prayer at the request of John's widow Yoko Ono. After the candlelit vigil in Liverpool, hundreds joined arms and sang Lennon's famous anti-war anthem *Give Peace A Chance*.

NATIONAL HEADLINES

1 March

Legendary Everton footballer Dixie Dean dies from heart failure, while watching a derby at his beloved Goodison Park.

27 March

123 oil rig workers are killed in the North Sea after the Alexander Kielland accommodation platform collapses.

3 August

Great Britain wins 21 Olympic medals in Moscow. The squad includes Merseysiders Joey Frost, Tony Willis, George Gilbody, Ray Gilbody and Keith Wallace.

21 September

RAF Greenham Common sees its first CND rally.

22 September

Three weeks of border clashes between Iran and Iraq finally erupt into all-out war.

17 October

The Queen makes history after becoming the first British monarch to make a state visit to the Vatican.

4 November

Ronald Reagan beats Jimmy Carter in a landslide victory to become the next president of the United States.

Top of the Pops

The Pretenders – *Brass in Pocket*
The Jam – *Going Underground*
The Police – *Don't Stand So Close To Me*
John Lennon – *Just Like Starting Over*
St Winifred's School Choir – *There's No One Quite Like Grandma*

memorable movies!

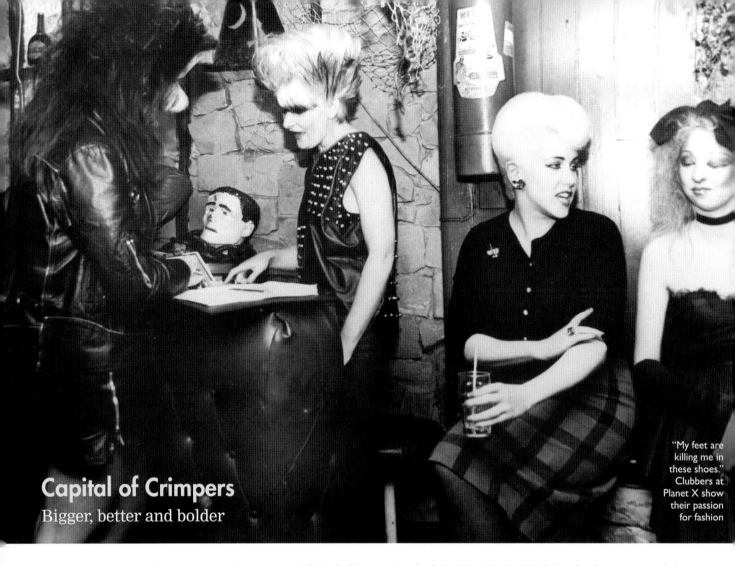

Capital of Crimpers
Bigger, better and bolder

"My feet are killing me in these shoes." Clubbers at Planet X show their passion for fashion

EVERYTHING about the '80s was over the top, especially in fashion.

From the New Romantics to Acid House, bigger was better – we had big hair, big shoulderpads, big sleeves, all in exaggerated shapes and sizes and bright colours.

Punk was the perfect outlet for the anti-establishment expression that young people were keen to convey. As the '80s wore on, the safety pins, tartan fabrics and pink hair were gradually replaced with the ruffled shirts, Victorian-style lacy cuffs and eyeliner of the New Romantics.

Planet X took over on the city's club scene where Eric's had left off, its clientele wearing outrageous outfits and high-maintenance, often high-rise, hairstyles, helping to make Liverpool the unofficial Capital of Crimpers.

Katherine Hamnett's oversized tops with large block letters

inspired the "Frankie Say" T-shirts that became one of the most iconic items of clothing for the decade.

The Levis adverts, including the famous launderette episode, triggered a craze not just for button-fly jeans, but for Doc Martens, white T-shirts and biker jackets. Teeny-boppers adorned their shoes with Grolsch bottle-tops and ripped up their jeans, much to mum's dismay.

For working women, the Eighties was time to wear the business suit – complete with the all-conquering shoulder pads. It was the decade of power dressing, when women aspired to look like Alexis Carrington and men wanted to be Crocket and Tubbs.

With the birth of the Soccer Casual, in came Lacoste tops, Pringle jumpers, Lois cords, Burberry scarves and Adidas Sambas. The label was the thing, and the more expensive and exclusive the better.

Frankie say ... buy our records. Phil Johnson, manager of a Church Street music store, gets behind the FGTH Two Tribes campaign

Razor sharp: BBC Radio Merseyside's Roger Hill, circa 1982

By George, a fashion look inspired no doubt by the Culture Club frontman

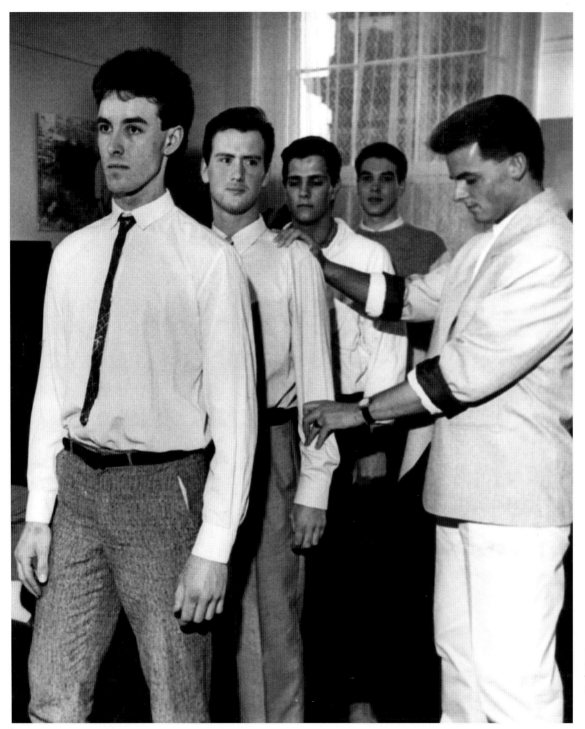

Hopes pinned on a career in fashion in 1986, even with those 'Miami Vice' rolled-up sleeves

November 1982 and a cold winter's day gives the perfect excuse to sport some furry legwarmers

Your crypt or mine? (Vlad's real name is actually Vincent)

Topsy-turvy temperatures
Fish forecast puts Britain in a spin

IT was the decade of raining men, walking on sunshine and a wind of change.

But nobody was singing on the morning of October 16, 1987, when Britain woke to find a trail of destruction left by gale-force winds – something that even Michael Fish had failed to see coming. The BBC's most famous forecaster will always be remembered for his notorious gaffe ahead of the Great Storm of 1987. Fish declared: "A lady rang the BBC and said she heard that there was a hurricane on the way. Well, don't worry if you're watching, there isn't."

Defending his position, the weatherman has always insisted he was not referring to the UK, but to Florida instead.

In January that same year, Britain's stiff upper lip had quivered under a European cold spell that brought public transport to a standstill.

In an editorial, The Daily Mail roared: "Russia copes. Scandinavia copes. Germany copes. Canada and the US cope. British Rail collapses."

Bizarrely, the Liverpool Echo reported that more Merseysiders than ever before were likely to be taking a skiing holiday that winter.

But in 1988, the sun shone on New Brighton Beach after Wirral Borough Council spent £15,000 adding 50,000 tons of sand onto the resort's foreshore. Who'd want to go abroad?

A victim of the gales – a lorry on its side on the Thelwall Viaduct on the M6

Surveying the rubble left after a chimney stack collapsed at a flat in Wallasey

Slush hour: City centre worker, Peter Whatman glides through the snow at Mount Pleasant

Early morning in the city centre in February 1985, and not a vehicle in sight

THE WEDDING OF THE DECADE

NATIONAL HEADLINES

29 March
Thousands of people jog through the normally quiet Sunday streets of the capital to compete in the first ever London marathon.

30 March
President Reagan is shot and wounded by a lone gunman in Washington.

4 April
Aldaniti, nursed back from career-threatening injury three times, wins a fairytale Grand National ridden by Bob Champion, who fought, and beat, cancer.

British group Bucks Fizz win the Eurovision Song Contest with 'Making Your Mind Up'.

22 May
Peter Sutcliffe is found guilty of being the 'Yorkshire Ripper'. He is sentenced to life.

5 July
Up to 30 police officers are injured as rioters take the streets of Toxteth.

29 September
Liverpool football legend Bill Shankly dies from a heart attack, aged 68.

Top of the Pops

Adam and the Ants – *Prince Charming*
Specials – *Ghost Town*
Soft Cell – *Tainted Love*
Shakin' Stevens – *This Ole House*
Human League – *Don't You Want Me*

LIVERPOOL has always been up for it when it comes to street parties and the wedding of Prince Charles and Lady Diana Spencer was no different.

1981 was a tale of two princes – Prince Charming, aka Adam Ant, who was swashbuckling his way to the top of the charts, and Prince Charles, who brought the nation to a standstill when he married Lady Spencer.

The Royal Wedding was undoubtedly the big story of the year and Diana's dress, designed by David and Elizabeth Emmanuel, was the fashion highlight. The couple were married on July 29 at St Paul's Cathedral before an invited congregation of 3,500 and an estimated global TV audience of 750 million – making it the most popular programme ever broadcast in the world at that point.

Britons enjoyed a national holiday to mark the great occasion.

The Return of the Great Adventure.

RAIDERS of the LOST ARK

memorable movies!

Nine days of hell
Chaos and violence rule the streets

WHEN police officers stopped a car just off Granby Street in Toxteth on a hot and sticky early evening in July 1981, little could they have realised that, within hours, Liverpool would be plunged into England's worst ever riots.

A crowd gathered around the scene in Selbourne Street and in the fracas that followed, three police officers were injured. That, though, was a curtain raiser for what was about to erupt in Toxteth. Unwittingly, the police officers and the watching crowd lit the touch paper to a chain of events that was to see dramatic pictures of a blazing Liverpool beamed across the world.

From July 4, it was to be nine days before peace was to be restored to Toxteth, but within those nine days, almost 1,000 police officers had been injured, 500 arrests had been made, 70 buildings had been destroyed by fire, massive looting had occurred and for the first time on the mainland, police had fired CS gas canisters in

a bid to disperse the crowds. At the height of the riots, black parents took to the battle-scarred streets in a bid to bring peace. They formed a peace patrol and toured the riot areas on foot with loud speakers.

The Rt Rev David Sheppard and the Most Rev Derek Worlock played a key role in restoring some sense of normality to a battered and broken community.

Sheppard summed up the reasons behind the riots when he said there were a series of separate human problems in the area – unemployment, housing, schools, a lack of facilities for recreation and sport. "People here have had a bad deal for a very long time," he said. "I am very conscious of the hurt to the whole community."

Margaret Thatcher responded by appointing one of her top men, Michael Heseltine, as Minister for Merseyside. Local people gave him the name Tarzan.

A milk float burns outside the Rialto

The ironic sign over the Pic N Pay at Lodge Lane, one of the shops looted during the riots

Michael Heseltine leads the way on the Yellow Submarine

All the fun of the fa
But this drumming
hard wo

Summer of fun

A bloomin' marvellous treat

THE weather smiled on Liverpool during the International Garden Festival year of 1984.

Born from the embers of the Toxteth Riots, the event at the reclaimed landfill site in Otterspool caught the imagination of people from near and far. Business boomed during the 166 days the festival was open and by the time it closed in the middle of October, 3.3 million visitors had flooded through the gates. Inside, all of them, many visiting and revisiting, found a magic land of entertainment and spectacle – and immense goodwill.

Not only had the festival been made out of nothing in record time, but crime, even of the pettiest sort, was nil. The festival got off to a blooming good start when it was opened by the Queen in May, amid stunning floral displays.

There was a Yellow Submarine, a dancing display, and trains that chuffed and whistled their way across the festival site.

The public visited the festival with enjoyment and pleasure, particularly the Scousers who were proud of what had been achieved on the banks of the Mersey.

An aerial view of
the International
Garden Festival site

Above: Jazz and
steel combo
Breakfast Time
drum up support

Hats off to fearless
lion tamer Mark Hollis

Ricky Tomlinson
is appointed
referee of the
'Yard of Ale'
competition

This Liverpool officer soon had the ladies laughing – and with a name like Sergeant Ken Dodd it's not hard to guess why

Ice cream fun for these girls at the Festival Gardens in May 1985

Blessed are we

Adoration for Pope

LIVERPOOL was certainly the place to visit in the Eighties, attracting friends from afar to the city.

Pope John Paul II received a magnificent Mersey welcome when he made his historic visit to the region in May 1982.

He arrived at Liverpool's Speke Airport to the amazing sight of more than 150,000 people gathered to give him a reception that even eclipsed those associated with the Beatles or a triumphant football team.

Flags and banners draped from every window along the eight-mile procession route and people thronging the roadside showed their adoration in song.

They gave the Pope a rousing chorus of the Kop anthem 'You'll Never Walk Alone' and 'We Love You John Paul We Do'.

The Pope took an hour to reach the city centre in his Popemobile, a specially adapted bullet-proof car, with bodyguards in close attendance.

As well as Royal visits from the Prince and Princess of Wales, and Princess Margaret, Liverpool welcomed pop royalty in 1984 as Paul McCartney returned to his home city. And in return he gave the city the first look at his film *Give My Regards To Broad Street* at the Odeon cinema.

The same year, Yoko Ono and Sean Lennon visited Liverpool – the pair played cat and mouse with the world's media as their limousine took them on a tour of Merseyside, which included John's old home in Menlove Avenue and a host of other Beatles' haunts.

"Liverpool is great. I always wanted to see it. My daddy said it was a nice place," said Sean.

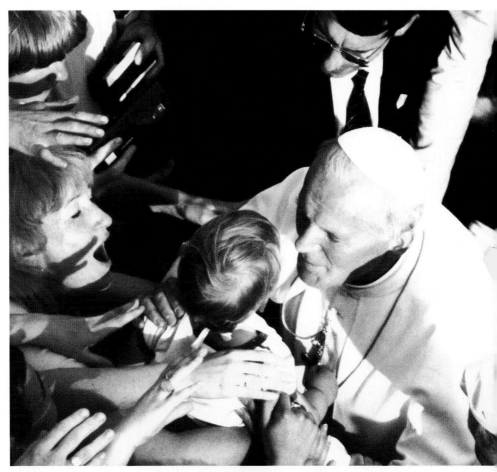

Crowds gather to see the Pope in May 1982

The Pope convoy makes its way down Hope Street

Blushing Princess Diana on a tour of the Halewood Ford factory. She laughed that, "The men have given me a hard time" with their wolf-whistles and cheers, but she seemed to enjoy every minute of her visit

Paul McCartney receives the Freedom of the city

Yoko Ono with Sean Lennon

A WAR WE HAD TO WIN

GENERAL Galtieri threw down the gauntlet to Britain when Argentina invaded the Falkland Islands in March 1982.

When the crisis ended 10 weeks later, more than 230 British lives had been lost, four warships sunk as well as one merchant ship, the Atlantic Conveyor.

Captain Ian North (pictured right) known affectionately on Merseyside as Captain Birds Eye, and Merseyside's Brian Williams received high honours for their service in the South Atlantic on the ill-fated container ship Atlantic Conveyor.

A posthumous Distinguished Service Cross went to Captain North, 59, for his brave leadership, and Third Engineer Mr Williams, of Bebington, Wirral, was awarded the Queen's Gallantry Medal for his courageous rescue bid after the ship was hit by two Exocet missiles. Captain North, the highly respected Cunard skipper, was the last man to leave the Liverpool-registered ship.

It was known that he got into the water and to a raft but he was never seen again. Survivor Mr Williams, 35, twice braved appalling smoke and heat in a bid to rescue a mechanic before being ordered to abandon ship.

NATIONAL HEADLINES

14 January

Mark Thatcher is found safe and well in the Sahara Desert, six days after going missing.

26 January

Unemployment in the UK reaches 3 million for the first time since the 1930s.

4 April

Geraldine Rees became the first woman jockey to complete the Grand National, finishing eighth aboard Cheers. The winner was Grittar, partnered by Dick Saunders.

14 June

White flags fly over Port Stanley as British troops finally end the Argentine rule.

21 June

Princess Diana gives birth to a baby boy, named William.

9 July

Michael Fagan breaks into Buckingham Palace and spends ten minutes talking to the Queen until he is apprehended.

7 October

Sue Townsend's novel 'The Secret Diary of Adrian Mole, Aged 13 and Three Quarters' is published.

Top of the Pops

Madness – *House of Fun*
Musical Youth – *Pass the Dutchie*
Dexy's Midnight Runners
– *Come On Eileen*
Survivor – *Eye of the Tiger*
Renee and Renato – *Save Your Love*

memorable movies!

He is afraid.
He is totally alone.
He is 3 million light years from home.

A STEVEN SPIELBERG FILM

E.T.

THE EXTRA-TERRESTRIAL

Echo and the Bunnymen enjoy a brew in their favourite dock road cafe

The sound and the fury

Mersey Beat back at the top

LIVERPOOL ruled the music scene once again in the 1980s – Mersey bands rocked, shocked and thrilled us all.

Echo and the Bunnymen, The Icicle Works, Dead Or Alive, The Teardrop Explodes, Flock of Seagulls, OMD, The Lotus Eaters, China Crisis, It's Immaterial, Pale Fountains, The Christians, Black, The Las, Half Man Half Biscuit, The Mighty Wah! . . . the list goes on and on.

Fragments of time frozen in precious and well-used 45s or 33 and a third rpm.

At one point in 1984 there were seven songs by Liverpool groups, including two from Frankie, in the Top Forty.

In 1983, FGTH were on the dole – by 1984 they had rewritten all the pop record books and shot to international stardom.

Stock, Aitken and Waterman struck gold with the Dead Or Alive single *You Spin Me Round (Like A Record)* and rocketed Rick Astley, Sonia and the Reynolds Girls into the charts.

Neighbours and Home and Away were well established Wizards from Oz, ensuring a whole crop of television soap stars would eventually invade this country.

In 1984, New Brighton Rock welcomed the likes of Madness and Spandau Ballet, while in 1986, it was the Albert Dock's turn with 'Rock Around The Dock'.

One of the biggest pop events on Merseyside was when superstar Michael Jackson entertained thousands of fans in a concert at Aintree racecourse in 1988.

Janice Long became the only female DJ to host Top of the Pops and every week we tuned in to hear John Peel's quips during the chart rundown: "At Number 18, it's Jennifer Rush, scoring more often than Ian Rush . . ."

Holly Johnson arrives at the Royal Court for a soundcheck, December 21, 1984

Pete Wylie

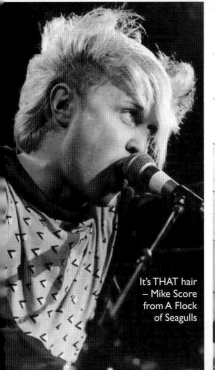

It's THAT hair – Mike Score from A Flock of Seagulls

OMD – Andy McCluskey and Paul Humphreys

Jayne Casey

25

Jason Donovan, breaking hearts in Quadrant Park, May 1989

The Damned at Rock Around The Dock, 1986

Fans try to get a glimpse of Sam Fox at HMV in March 1986

Don't forget your Kylie T-shirt when you visit the Hit Man Road Show

Left: The excitement builds for Michael Jackson's arrival at Aintree in 1988

Y? TS

Get on the bus get out of Doledrum

THE economy of Merseyside collapsed with an almighty crash in the 1970s and early 1980s, seeing tens of thousands of people joining a dole queue that grew by the day.

Industrial giants that were household names closed or drastically reduced their workforces, in an epidemic that saw at least 200,000 jobs being lost.

Dunlop, Meccano, Tate and Lyle, the docks, English Electric, British Leyland – a never-ending list of casualties.

In a short space of time, Liverpool's manufacturing base, and all of those unskilled jobs, virtually disappeared.

On January 26, 1982, Merseyside unemployment figures, 131,320, were reported to be the worst since the war.

Many of the middle-class who came out of college in the early 1980s went into well-paid jobs in finance, the media, law, and property development. But Thatcher's Britain offered little for young people in Liverpool and hundreds of thousands went straight from school to the dole.

Others went on to the government's Youth Training Scheme for 16 and 17 year olds, working full-time for £27.50 a week. Many frowned upon the YTS scheme as an excuse for cheap labour, with participants learning little more than how to make cups of tea or sweep the floor.

But for some, it opened up a new world of creative opportunities. Liverpool Council even topped up YTSers' money to trade union rates, and offered a guaranteed job at the end of the scheme.

Tate & Lyle workers
arrive for a mass
meeting in January
1981 – the younger
ones can smile

A fireman cools
down on Lodge Lane

29

Birds Eye workers hang their hats in 1989

Master of the Marina:
Bill Broadbent at the
South Docks in 1987

Stephen West's mammoth
task in 1987 was to 'paper
and paint' this huge
concrete silo at Allied
Mills near Seaforth

SIX TINY MIRACLES

JANET Walton, 32, gave birth to sextuplets – all girls – at Liverpool's Oxford Street Maternity Hospital on November 18, 1983.

Mrs Walton, who lived with husband Graham in Wallasey, had taken a course of fertility drugs before conceiving. The girls were born by Caesarean section between 7.56pm and 8pm. There was a 15-strong team in the operating theatre. The babies were born eight weeks short of full-term pregancy, a compromise worked out to give Janet the least health risk and the babies the best chance of survival. The babies were named Hannah Jane, Jennifer Rose, Lucy Anne, Kate Elizabeth, Ruth Michelle and Sarah Louise. Little Ruth was the last of the sextuplets, who quickly became world-famous, to go home from hospital to join her sisters, in January, 1984.

The Waltons were overwhelmed at the way the nation showered gifts on their instant family, which quickly thrived.

memorable movies!

Something happens when she hears the music... It's her freedom. It's her fire. It's her life.

Flashdance

What a feeling.

Take your passion and make it happen!

NATIONAL HEADLINES

17 January
Britons switch on to watch BBC's new Breakfast Time show, presented by Frank Bough and Selina Scott.

28 January
Rock and roll star Billy Fury dies, aged 42.

31 January
A new law rules that all car drivers and front seat passengers must wear seatbelts.

9 February
A nationwide hunt begins for the racing horse Shergar, after the prize stallion is kidnapped from stables in County Kildare.

21 April
The one-pound coin is introduced in England and Wales.

9 June
Margaret Thatcher wins a landslide victory by a margin large enough to guarantee a full five-year second term as Prime Minister of Britain.

2 October
Neil Kinnock is elected leader of the Labour Party.

2 December
Michael Jackson's music video for 'Thriller', directed by John Landis, is broadcast for the first time.

Top of the Pops

Men At Work – *Down Under*
David Bowie – *Let's Dance*
Billy Joel – *Uptown Girl*
Culture Club (pictured) – *Karma Chameleon*
The Flying Pickets – *Only You*

The biggest spring clean on Merseyside gets under way at Albert Dock

The road to glory
City gems sparkle again

TWO of the most important developments in Liverpool during the 1980s were the Albert Dock village and Cavern Walks.

In 1984, business was soon booming at Cavern Walks, in Mathew Street. A £40,000 life-size bronze statue of the Beatles was erected in the centre of the complex of shops.

The luxury development featured trailing plants, vaulted ceilings and tinted glass. More than 15,000 bricks were removed intact from the old Cavern Club and incorporated into the Cavern Walks scheme, forming arches reminiscent of those in the original venue.

Albert Dock was originally built to accommodate sailing ships with up to 1,000 tons of cargo capacity but by the turn of the century only 7 per cent of ships using the port were

sailing ships. The dock's days were numbered and it was finally closed in 1972.

Plans for the refurbishment of Albert Dock were prepared in 1982, work began in 1983 and the first phase was opened in 1984 in time for the arrival of the Tall Ships Race and the International Garden Festival.

On May 24, 1988, Prince Charles performed the official reopening ceremony for the transformed Albert Dock complex, following in the footsteps of his great great-great-grandfather Prince Albert, who had opened the original dock bearing his name in 1846.

The £50m conversion turned the Albert Dock into a unique museum, arts, leisure, shops and office complex, and made it the jewel in Liverpool's crown.

Steve Knox clears away some of the grass covering the old cobblestones at the Albert Dock, April 1982

33

Before the makeover: Photographed from the site of the Maritime Museum in July 1980

Tommy Steele unveils the Eleanor Rigby statue on Stanley Street

"ALL THE LONELY PEOPLE..."
This statue was sculptured and donated to the City of Liverpool by Tommy Steele as a tribute to the Beatles. The casting was sponsored by the Liverpool Echo.
DECEMBER 1982

Gerry Marsden
and Noel Edmonds
at The Albert
Dock, filming
Noel's TV show
Time Of Your Life

The 'melting' process – demolition on the
South Docks Grain Silo, as the site is
cleared for a housing development in 1989

Mike McCartney joins in a duet with Paul, unveiling the statue in 1984

Coffee and cream cakes while Smith and Johnson play for their supper in Cavern Walks

Reach for the skies: CATS flying school

The youngest and oldest
set out for Paris aboa
Concorde on April 6, 1985
Mr William Woodwood
West Derby who w
celebrating his 71st birthd
and one-year-old L
Thompson of Huyto

Trip of a lifetime

Supersonic style

THE Eighties was a period of ups and downs for Liverpool Airport, but one supersonic visitor always led by the nose.

Concorde graced the apron at Speke many times, bringing guests in style for the world's most famous horse race at Aintree. The Liverpool Echo chartered the supersonic jet in 1984 as part of the Grand National celebrations and in 1988 made history when 1,000 readers flew on Concorde from Liverpool Airport – the highest ever number of passengers to fly on the craft in a single day.

The first transatlantic flight to land at Speke was in October 1986 when Concorde touched down in Liverpool from New York. Originally the flight was due to touch down at Manchester, but so many Scousers were aboard that it was decided to travel door-to-door.

Back on terra firma, Jimmy Saville declared it 'The Age of the Train' as the Intercity 125 was the pride of Britain's railways, boasting hi-tech sliding doors, microwave kitchens and a speed exceeded only in Japan.

Jaguar was king of the road thanks to high sales in the US and the quest among American motorists for something quintessentially British.

And who can forget Clive Sinclair's most famous invention – perhaps for all the wrong reasons.

On reviewing the electric C5 in 1985, Moya Jones comments in the Liverpool Echo: "It would be great fun in the sun-baked prom at Benidorm, or tootling round the paths of a holiday camp. But in peak hour traffic, in Dale Street, negotiating a busy car park at the local hypermarket – not for me."

Arriving in style – Simon O'Brien, Ann Diamond, Bill Dean, Debbie Greenwood and Russell Grant

A National knees-up: Peter Hewitt, Faith Brown and Barbara Windsor

POPULAR

Sam Toy, manager of the Ford Halewood plant, in 1980

Electric dreams:
Test driving the
Sinclair C5

Soap stars: Staff at Lime
Street celebrate the
station being named
the third cleanest in
Britain in 198

RELAX . . . WE'RE NUMBER 1 AGAIN

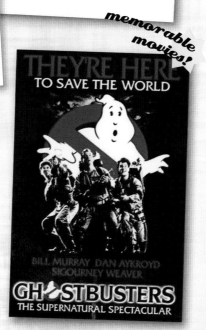

NATIONAL HEADLINES

14 February

Jayne Torvill and Christopher Dean scoop the gold medal for Olympic ice skating in Sarajevo, Yugoslavia.

12 March

Thousands of Britain's miners go on strike, in protest against pit closures.

7 July

Martina Navratilova wins her fifth Wimbledon singles title.

11 August

South African-born British athlete Zola Budd collides with Mary Decker during the women's 3,000m race at the Los Angeles Olympics.

4 September

Thomas the Tank Engine and Friends is first broadcast on television.

12 October

A massive bomb at the Grand Hotel in Brighton during the Conservative Party conference kills three people and injures several leading Tories.

15 December

Band Aid's recording of *Do They Know It's Christmas?* organised by Bob Geldof and Midge Ure, shoots to number one in the singles chart.

Top of the Pops

Paul McCartney – *Pipes of Peace*
Nena – *99 Red Balloons*
George Michael – *Careless Whisper*
Stevie Wonder – *I Just Called*
Duran Duran – *The Reflex*

WELCOME TO THE PLEASUREDOME

memorable movies!

THEY'RE HERE
TO SAVE THE WORLD

BILL MURRAY   DAN AYKROYD
SIGOURNEY WEAVER

GHOSTBUSTERS
THE SUPERNATURAL SPECTACULAR

IT WAS a case of "bought the single, bought the T-shirt" in 1984 when Liverpool group Frankie Goes to Hollywood had its first big hit.

Frankie's first three singles, *Relax*, *Two Tribes* and *The Power of Love* all went to number one and so did their debut album *Welcome To The Pleasure Dome* – a feat never achieved by any other group in pop history.

The band became only the second act in the history of the UK charts to reach number one with their first three singles – the first being Gerry & the Pacemakers in 1964.

Frankie began in controversy, which seemed to follow them around. Relax was banned by Radio 1 – and the ban sent the single soaring to the top of the charts. The band went on to defy critics who said they could not play live, with a stunning American debut tour that had the crowds screaming for more.

The man in black
Opening hearts and minds

THE black outfit, his urchin-kids in tow, Yosser Hughes, Alan Bleasdale's creation, was one of the most-striking figures of the '80s, as Merseyside talent – writing and acting – dominated television.

Boys From The Blackstuff won a Bafta for actor Bernard Hill in 1982 – creating a memorable catchphrase "Gizza job" – and established Bleasdale as one of our greatest TV dramatists.

But Liverpool was making even more inroads elsewhere on the box.

Brookside, provisionally called Meadowcroft, changed the concept of soap opera in Britain.

Launching in 1982, it was the creation of Phil Redmond who had bought a housing estate to add extra authenticity to his dream. Redmond was also behind the introduction of Grange Hill's original Scouser Ziggy, "To show people there's life north of Watford."

Jim Hitchmough's ITV series Watching, ruled by Liverpool people, humour and values, was described as being "a cross between The Liver Birds and Letter To Brezhnev", brimming with wit.

Cilla Black received 170,000 letters during the first series of Surprise Surprise in 1984 and there were a Lorra Lorra love rats watching in the wings when Blind Date made Cilla an LWT living legend.

Scouser Kate Robbins went on to impersonate Ms Black when she added her vocal virtuosity to the latex lampooners of Spitting Image.

Carla Lane made a crust with the arrival of the Boswells in the successful sit-com, Bread.

And Alexei Sayle's Stuff vied with Harry Enfield in the fresh and exciting comedy ratings war.

On Radio Merseyside, one of the most popular shows ever to hit the airwaves arrived – Hold Your Plums. Billy Butler, of The Tuxedos band and Thank Your Lucky Stars fame, teamed up with Wally Scott for a show of unique Scouse wit.

Bernard Hill as Yosser Hughes

Paul and Linda McCartney join the cast of Bread in October 1988

Tom O'Connor and family, pictured in 1987

Blind Date host Cilla Black with contestants Alex Tatham and Sue Middleton in 1988 – the pair were married in 1991. Picture courtesy of London Weekend Television

Emma Wray and
Paul Brown in
Watching.
Picture courtesy of
Granada Television

Hold Your
Plums –
Billy Butler

Sporting a suitable
seabird on her hat ...
Janice Long gets set for
the Radio 1 Roadshow in
Southport, July 17, 1984

The Brookside boys – Simon O'Brien, Ricky Tomlinson, Jason Hope and Brian Regan, 1987

Tearing up the script
Class divide deals a reality cheque

AT the turn of the decade, half of all married women in Britain had swopped the kitchen for the office.

It was the decade of the supermarket, microwaves and ready meals. Everyone saved for a mortgage – including council house tenants who could buy their homes for the first time. Those who got rich on the back of a property boom had really never had it so good.

Society and community, apparently, were dead. But how could a place which survived on community spirit ever come to terms with the ideals of those who genuinely believed "there was no such thing as society"?

Charles and Di's wedding brightened the gloom of lengthening dole queues and hairdressers did a roaring trade in Di lookalike styles. Eighties man watched the first televised snooker match – eighties woman watched Brideshead Revisited. Sky television went up and the Berlin wall came down. The Falklands conflict sparked a spirit of wartime camaraderie. We reckoned we'd never get used to seat belts and the one-pound coin and moaned about wheelclamps and Boy George.

Smokers started to become society's outcasts as cinemas went multi-screen and refused to provide ashtrays.

As the 1980s came of age, sterling rallied against the dollar and women could go for free computerised screening for cervical cancer. A wind of change was blowing – we sipped Perrier and talked of Perestroika. Kids knew if they didn't drink their milk, they'd end up playing for Accrington Stanley. On the restaurant scene, delicate Nouvelle Cuisine arrived – we'd wait for the next course to turn up, which it never did, and then nip home via the chippie.

Gizza job: The 500-long queue outside Old Swan Job Centre in 1983

A microwave might put a ping in your step, but you can't beat a pot of Scouse

47

Quiet please: Filming 'Bread' in Dingle, but for shift worker Ian Dean the Boswells are crumby neighbours who stop him sleeping during the day

Eyes down: The Top Rank bingo club in Dingle

RAISING MILLIONS FOR AFRICA

NATIONAL HEADLINES

1 January

The first British mobile phone call is made.

3 March

Miners' leaders end their year-long strike without any peace deal. Arthur Scargill says the campaign against job losses will continue.

11 March

Mikhail Gorbachev becomes Soviet leader.

11 May

56 football supporters are killed and 256 injured after a fire engulfed the Bradford City Football Stadium. It is the worst fire disaster in the history of British football.

29 May

39 football fans are killed at the Heysel Stadium in Brussels, the darkest hour in the history of the UEFA competitions.

7 July

Boris Becker wins Wimbledon aged just 17.

1 October

Police in riot gear close off areas of Toxteth after riots erupt in Liverpool.

Top of the Pops

Madonna – *Into the Groove*
Jennifer Rush – *The Power of Love*
Dead or Alive – *You Spin Me Right Round*
Paul Hardcastle – *19*
Shakin' Stevens – *Merry Christmas Everyone*

"GIVE us your f****** money now!"

It is one of the passionate phrases that made Bob Geldof a household name in 1985 when the dishevelled-looking, sleep-neglected Irishman and former Boomtown Rat frontman pleaded with people not to go out to the pub that night but stay in at home, watch a pop concert on telly and to donate the money that was not spent on booze to feeding the world instead.

July 13, 1985, was a magical day when Status Quo opened up a thunderous Live Aid concert in Wembley Stadium that seemed to get better and better with each world famous act – Paul McCartney, Bono, Queen, Sting, Elton John and Dire Straits.

In Liverpool, The Empire hosted its own charity fundraiser for Ethiopia called Liver Aid. The line-up included Black, It's Immaterial, The Christians, The Lotus Eaters, Icicle Works, Liverpool Express, Electric Morning, Fragile Friends, The Searchers and Lawnmower.

memorable movies!

49

Mersey tide of protest

Fighting for the future

A HUGE wave of protest swept Liverpool on November 29, 1980, as thousands of marchers poured into the city to demonstrate against rising unemployment.

From the length and breadth of Britain, trade unionists, Labour Party officials, supporters and the unemployed, swept through Liverpool with Michael Foot's army. So massive was this demonstration – claimed by organisers at more than 100,000 – that when the front reached Pier Head for the rally, there were still an estimated 15,000 waiting to leave Sefton Park, one hour 40 minutes after the march began.

For four years during the 1980s, Liverpool became a virtual republic of People Power, with Militant Derek Hatton at the helm. The clash between the city and the Government led to a flood of adverse publicity about Liverpool, its politics and its people.

Although it was the Militants dominating the headlines, there were only a handful of Militant members serving as councillors.

The rest supported the stand being made to bring jobs and services and to build new homes. The left-wing Labour council of the 1980s was hugely supported across the city, with turn-outs at local elections well over the 50 per cent mark.

In 1984, Lime Street saw the People's Festival – some called it the People's Propaganda, others said it would not work. But on that day, 50,000 people turned up and Merseyside County Council declared themselves, "Very happy." The aim was to unite Merseyside against the threat of the abolition of the county council, but on the day, the people seemed to matter more than the words.

In the middle of all the politics strode, side by side, the city's two church leaders, Roman Catholic Archbishop Derek Worlock, and his close Anglican friend Bishop David Sheppard, who spoke up for the city and its people at every opportunity.

Left: Michael Foot, Leader of the Labour Party, seems bemused by some of the delegation from the Peoples March or Jobs outside the Commons in 1981

Right: Thousands of demonstraters march from Sefton park to he Pier Head in 1981

51

John Hamilton and
Derek Hatton lead
the marchers in 1984

The People's Festival

Above: Clowning around at the People's Festival in 1984

The Sam Bond affair: Liverpool Council's race relations officer

Archbishop Warlock and Bishop Sheppard in Hope Street, January 1984

Mash it up!
Riding the gravy train

THE days of mashed potato scooped out like ice cream and 'dolloped' on dinner plates throughout Liverpool's school canteens was gradually coming to an end.

It was a case of "chips with everything." Even your roast dinner if you were unlucky. And these were whoppers . . . way before the micro chip (the microwave version and the IT variety) came along.

Spam Fritters were a tasty revolution, but nothing could halt the ever-reliable appearance of lukewarm custard and stodgy rhubarb pie. Many schoolkids rebelled with their dinner money by escaping out, ironically for chips to the local chippie, and to wash it all down with a 'frozen' orange Jubilee or Mambo – a delicacy in triangle cardboard consisting of mushy ice.

Scouse could be had in the canteen but it was never as good as your ma made. It was time to educate us all on nutrition and no-one had even heard of Jamie Oliver. Two talented football players were looking after their teenage diets: Robbie Fowler and Tony Grant – both were doing well for Liverpool Schoolboys playing their hearts out at their home ground in Penny Lane.

Television's Grange Hill featured characters who were as inventive as Vivienne Westwood when it came to schoolie wear. Life indeed mirrored art as school uniforms were going through a transformation.

Thirty years after St Trinian's created "the schoolie", punk and New Romantic influences ensured that kids would be sent home from school for wearing make-up. And the girls, too. School ties became an iconic fashion accessory – what you did with that piece of cloth around your neck could put you in a class of your own.

Margaret Orme and her choice of meals at Notre Dame High School, January 1984

Dinner time at the Roscommon Street Junior School in Liverpool, 1989

Le crunch – sampling the delights of Liverpool school dinners, a party of under-14s from Rennes, France, visit Dovecot Community School for lunch in 1988

Angelic children from Toxteth Primary pray at morning assembly

Swotting for O-Level

Can we wash your fire engine mister? The 9th Fairfield Scout Group call into Speke Airport for National Scout Job Week, 1989

Policemen are getting younger these days

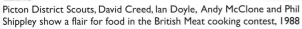

Picton District Scouts, David Creed, Ian Doyle, Andy McClone and Phil Shippley show a flair for food in the British Meat cooking contest, 1988

Green fingers at Anfield Nursery, 1984

How's that for harmony – local policemen enjoy a game of cricket with youngsters in Parliament Street

58

THE GREATEST DERBY IN THE WORLD

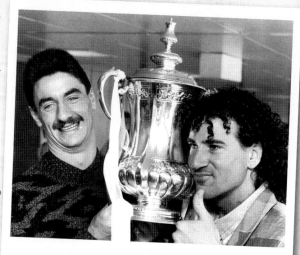

WE think it's the greatest derby in the world – and in 1986 it was underlined just why.

Liverpool and Everton were, without question, the two finest sides in the country when they met for the first time in an FA Cup final at Wembley on Saturday, May 10, 1986.

And in Ian Rush and Gary Lineker they had two marksmen who were the envy of Europe. Having already surrendered their league title to Kenny Dalglish's Liverpool, Everton were determined to deny their rivals the "double."

Everton's England striker Gary Lineker struck first with his 40th goal of the season.

But Liverpool proved that if you offer them an inch, they will take a mile by taking advantage of sudden sloppiness to equalise through Rush. Everton's spirits sank and further goals from Craig Johnston and Rush again clinched Liverpool's first ever league and FA Cup double. That season, the Mersey rivals also met in the Charity Shield, the two-legged Screen Sport Super Cup final, a goalless draw at Goodison in the league, a League Cup tie at Goodison won by Ian Rush, and another league game at Anfield where Liverpool postponed Everton's title celebrations with a 3-1 win.

NATIONAL HEADLINES

9 January
Defence Secretary Michael Heseltine resigns after a row with the Prime Minister over the Westland affair.

28 January
The American space shuttle Challenger explodes after take-off, killing all seven astronauts on board.

3 February
The Pope meets Mother Theresa in Calcutta, at her refuge for the sick and dying.

1 March
The government launches its Aids awareness campaign with the slogan "Aids: Don't die of ignorance."

28 April
The Soviet Union acknowledges there has been a major accident at the Chernobyl nuclear power plant in Ukraine.

22 June
England's World Cup hopes end in the quarter finals with a 2-1 defeat to Argentina.

23 July
Prince Andrew and Sarah Ferguson are married at Westminster Abbey.

Top of the Pops

It's Immaterial – *Driving Away From Home*
Billy Ocean – *When the Going Gets Tough*
Communards – *Don't Leave Me This Way*
Spitting Image – *The Chicken Song*
Jackie Wilson – *Reet Petite*

memorable movies!

United in grief
Football's darkest hour

HEYSEL and Hillsborough. Two catastrophes costing a total of 135 lives which changed the world of football and how the world perceived its supporters.

But who could have imagined that Liverpool fans would have been central to both of them?

The first left them universally reviled and the other, four years later, won them global sympathy – this time as the victims, despite the efforts of a certain national newspaper to prove otherwise.

John Wark watches as Juventus parade the trophy around the Heysel Stadium

An injured soccer fan is assisted off the Hillsborough pitch by a policeman and a Liverpool supporter

John Aldridge lays flowers with his daughter at Anfield

Screen with envy

A letter to the world

THE Liverpool voice, personality and talent were well and truly stamped on the small and big screen in the Eighties.

Stage success allowed our writers, actors, producers and directors a chance to develop in other genres.

Former teachers-turned-stage writers Alan Bleasdale and Willy Russell showed their talent for storytelling and sparkling dialogue.

Bleasdale created the dark, but very funny, No Surrender in 1989, where Protestant and Catholic clubs book the same hall on the same night.

Willy ensured his Everyman hits Educating Rita and Shirley Valentine became box office smashes with Julie Walters (1983) and Pauline Collins (1989) gaining wide critical acclaim. And, of course, Blood Brothers born in 1983

went on to become a worldwide hit. Fresh from TV success, Alan Bleasdale went on to write a stage musical Are You Lonesome Tonight? based on the life of Elvis Presley and played by Martin Shaw.

Former Everyman Theatre admin assistant by day and actress by night, Cathy Tyson honed her craft at the Hope Street venue and then RSC and landed a role in the film Mona Lisa before a succession of TV series.

The surprise film hit of the '80s was Letter To Brezhnev, a low budget, but spirited tale of two Scouse girls in a bid to escape their drudgery in Kirkby. It made stars of Margi Clarke and Alexandra Pigg and set writer Frank Clarke – Margi's brother – and director Chris Bernard onto successful film careers.

Left: Superwoman (Joan Turner) and Winnie (Gabrielle Daye) contemplate the growing chaos around them in No Surrender

Master of horror: Clive Barker

Cathy Tyson

Arriving in style
for the northern
charity premiere
of The Chain at
The Odeon in '85,
Willy Russell,
Barbara Dickson
and Bernard Hill

Peter Firth and
Alexandra Pigg in
Letter To Brezhnev

The McGann brothers:
From left, Mark, Steve, Joe and Paul

RIOT AT THE ROYAL COURT

BEASTIE mania was set to sweep England by storm in 1987 as the most outrageous and controversial group to emerge since the Sex Pistols toured the country.

The American hip-hop trio – whose hits included *Fight For Your Right To Party* and *No Sleep Till Brooklyn* – were starting to enjoy a high profile in the national press.

But the Beastie Boys gig at the Royal Court in Liverpool on May 30, 1987, made the national headlines for all the wrong reasons.

Trouble flared up and bottles, rubbish and even seats were thrown around the venue. It was a near riot. The Beastie Boys decided that enough was enough and left the stage as the police moved in with CS gas.

Merseyside Police later brought Beastie Boy Adam Horowitz back to Liverpool from London for questioning. Horowitz, better known to fans as Ad-Rock, appeared at Liverpool magistrates court in November 1987 accused of throwing a can of beer at a female fan, but was found innocent of the assault.

NATIONAL HEADLINES

6 March

193 people die after the Herald of Free Enterprise capsizes just outside the Belgian port of Zeebrugge.

11 June

Margaret Thatcher celebrates her third General Election win.

30 June

Peter Beardsley becomes the most expensive player transferred when he moves from Newcastle United to Liverpool for £1.9 million.

19 August

16 people are shot dead in Hungerford by lone gunman Michael Ryan.

16 October

Britain is battered by hurricane winds of up to 110mph.

19 October

Black Monday – the world's stock market collapses after shares on Wall Street suffer a wave of panic selling.

18 November

31 people die in a fire at King's Cross Station in London.

Top of the Pops

Black – *Wonderful Life*
Ferry Aid – *Let It Be*
T'Pau – *China In Your Hand*
Rick Astley – *Never Gonna Give You Up*
Pet Shop Boys – *Always On My Mind*

memorable movies!

We're the greatest!
The road to Wembley

The sign of success:
An open top bus tour of the city
for EFC with their Euoprean and
domestic silverware in 1985

THE Eighties was the Golden Age of Merseyside football with silver-lined seasons of unbroken success as Everton finally followed Liverpool's example and reeled in an impressive trophy haul.

The Blues came out of the shadows in 1984, winning the FA Cup, the Charity Shield and the FA Youth Cup.

For years, a Wembley derby had been the impossible dream. But on March 24, 1984, the Mersey rivals met at Wembley in the Milk Cup final. That historic 'Friendly Final' showpiece provided an excuse for a city-wide celebration. Street parties were staged back in Liverpool, while North London became a temporary vehicle for Scouse civic pride.

It was the same at the 1986 FA Cup final. The whole of Merseyside was full of excitement and the city centre a confusion of red and blue with market stalls selling flags,

rosettes, T-shirts and other souvenirs. This was the game everyone on Merseyside wanted to watch.

London was invaded by Scousers, who poured down the motorway, red and blue scarves hanging out of car and coach windows.

Everton and Liverpool never strayed too far from Wembley in the Eighties, the Reds monopolising the League Cup in its various guises and the Blues appearing in four FA Cup finals.

The success continued for manager Howard Kendall and his men when Everton clinched the championship in 1985.

And they won the European Cup Winners' Cup final the same year, beating Rapid Vienna 3-1 in Rotterdam.

Everton had won their first European trophy and 100 million viewers throughout the Continent watched them win in style.

True Blues: Brothers Ian and David Scothern

Starting at the top: The first Wembley for fans Elaine Seville and Michelle Meadows

The 1984 Milk Cup final

The LFC coach reaches
Lime Street with the
European Cup in 1984

GOODNIG
VIENNA
IT'S SCOUS
NOT STRAUS

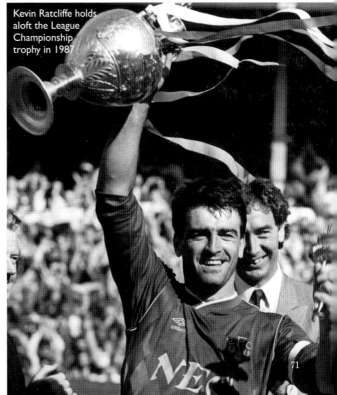

Kevin Ratcliffe holds aloft the League Championship trophy in 1987

71

All done up
for the big day

The front room balcony
makes a good viewing
point on Queens Drive

COMIC CAPERS FOR RED NOSE DAY

NATIONAL HEADLINES

24 May

The Prince of Wales officially reopens the Albert Dock.

15 June

The British government expresses growing concern over Acid House music and its effect on young people, during the 'Second Summer of Love'.

28 July

Paddy Ashdown is elected leader of the Liberal Democrats.

11 September

Pop star Michael Jackson brings the Bad tour to wow the crowds at Aintree.

27 September

Sprinter Ben Johnson is stripped of his Olympic gold medal after testing positive for drugs.

3 December

Health minister Edwina Currie provokes outrage by announcing that most of Britain's eggs are infected with salmonella.

21 December

Pan Am Flight 103 explodes over the Scottish town of Lockerbie, killing a total of 270 people.

RED Nose Day was born in 1988 and Merseyside was going crazy with raising funds for Comic Relief along with the rest of the country.

The very first Red Nose Day on Friday, February 5, 1988, raised a whacking £15 million. On BBC television, the whole evening was given over to Lenny Henry, Griff Rhys Jones and Jonathan Ross, presenting the primetime spectacular, viewed by more than 30 million people.

Pictured above, children of St Cleopas School in Toxteth celebrate the Red Nose Day fun in 1988, and above, bringing a smile to the dentist's chair, Julie Goodier and Carolann Watts.

memorable movies!

Top of the Pops

Wet Wet Wet – *With A Little Help From My Friends*
U2 – *Desire*
Yazz – *The Only Way Is Up*
Kylie Minogue – *I Should Be So Lucky*
Cliff Richard – *Mistletoe and Wine*

Battle of the Bots
Gift frenzy for top guns

Lewis's toy department, 1984

THEY were ugly and they were expensive.

But Cabbage Patch dolls become one of the most coveted toys on earth during the early 1980s.

Near-riots were reported in toy shops at Christmas as parents and children fought over each new delivery. The appeal of the pudgy-faced dolls was that each was, in some small way, unique – a computerised manufacturing process introduced little differences between each one – and rather than buying one, you adopted it.

For the boys, robots were all the rage in the 1980s – especially if you could transform into a nuclear explosive or perhaps more practically, a tin-opener.

Bill and Marj Lennon ran Buchanans toy shop, later known as Amazing Toys & Bikes, on County Road, Walton for 35 years until their retirement. In 1984 they managed to get their hands on Optimus Prime when other toy shops in Liverpool couldn't.

"At the time everyone in the country seemed to be after the Optimus Prime Transformer but most places had sold out," Marj recalled. "Suddenly one of our suppliers rang us up and he had about 100 and asked us if we wanted them.

"It was just 10 days before Christmas and we heard that Phil Easton on Radio City wanted one. We called him up and he announced on air that we had the toys.

"Well, all hell broke loose. It was like a scene from Starsky & Hutch with cars screeching up outside. We had queues right out of the front door!"

Amanda Nash in her bedroom crammed full of Barbie dolls and accessories, 1989

Freeport freedom
The wind in their sails

THE Tall Ships in 1984 brought a picturesque chapter of Liverpool's rich maritime past to life.

Some 60 square riggers, schooners and barques sailed into Albert Dock in July, followed by four days of shipboard public visits and crews' entertainment. On August 4, in the great Parade of Sail, the queens of the sea were dressed in all their finery, and glided down the river and dipped their flags in royal salute as they passed the Queen and Prince Philip on board Britannia. More than a million people watched in wonder.

A new age for Liverpool's North Docks beckoned in the 1980s. Discussing in 1983 the 'glimmer of hope' that Freeport status might offer, The Liverpool Echo commented: "This idea is just what Merseyside needs to get back on its feet – the chance to create real wealth instead of relying on a few more state handouts for our communal begging bowl. It is a tough challenge, but they must not fail us."

In 1984, the Mersey Docks and Harbour Company were sailing on the crest of a wave, when the 650-acre Freeport zone finally got the official go ahead from the government.

Merseyside was an outsider in the tough race for a Freeport, but it became a winner.

The spectacular Polish vessel
Dar Mlodziezy in full sail

Sale of the century at Liverpool's Freeport in 1988, as buyers from all over the world made tracks to the open-air auction site to scoop up the machines that built the Falkland Islands airport

Crowds wave to the Sir Thomas Sopwith at the 1985 River Pageant

HMS Liverpool, Midshipman Andy Collier meets Thomas and Beth from Crosby

All the nice
girls love a sailor:
HMS Liverpool

Sightseers gather to watch as the oil rig Sovereign Explorer makes its way up the Mersey